Self-help Yourself

(Find your "kick-ass" Mentor in a Self-help Book;

Follow the principles and create your better life)

OLIVE ROSE STEELE

Copyright © 2012 Olive Rose Steele
All rights reserved.
ISBN: 9781519062819
Published in 2016
Sketch by Gabriella Faith Laing
Self-help Yourself
(Find your "kick-ass" Mentor in a Self-help Book; follow the principles and create your better life)

THIS BOOK IS DEDICATED TO ...
My Faithful Readers.

Praise for Self-Help Yourself

"Self-Help Yourself" is very empowering; it gives you the ability to say "I can do whatever I set my mind to". This book allows me to rethink my priorities, it helps me to have greater self-esteem, morals, and other attributes, which will increase dignity and self-respect.
—Henry Reid

A nice presentation of step-by-step strategies to building personal resource, internal strength and resilience. There is a simultaneous wit and poignancy in the writing that uplifts and motivates the reader. This manual is a terrific resource.
—Sharon Lee

Another dynamic read!
—Tori Maartin

CONTENTS

Acknowledgments   i

Introduction

1	How's your life going?	Pg #4
2	My story	Pg #7
3	What is Self-Help?	Pg #10
4	Who needs Self-Help?	Pg #16
5	Why Self-Help?	Pg #30
6	When do I need Self-Help?	Pg #33
7	Where does Self-Help come from?	Pg #37
8	Self-Help should not be…	Pg #40
9	Self-Help should be…	Pg #42
10	Study Up	Pg #44
11	You got it	Pg #48

ACKNOWLEDGMENTS

I acknowledge Sam, Henry, Mary, Janice, Marva and Michael; and all the folks who ask: *What is Self-Help?* I hope the answers I give in this book will be helpful.

INTRODUCTION

You're drawn to this book by the title: **Self-help yourself** *(Find your "kick-ass" Mentor in a Self-help Book; follow the principles and create your better life)*.

Good.

Are you stressed-out? Want to hone a skill? Having relationships problems? Do you feel like you are wedged in a rut? Don't be frustrated. Answers to these and other questions are available… self-help yourself.

I will share what I know about the self-help way to change your life. Also, I will give you some suggestions to improve your confidence, self-worth, self-esteem, stature and gain favor.

This is a bold attempt on my part for though I acknowledge self-help as necessary for personal growth, I recognize some folks will pull back from the idea.

Self-help can set you free from having to map out your own plans to deal with angst, worries, and self-doubt.

You don't have to go hungry to lose the ten pounds you've been struggling with. Self-help books, audio tapes, CDs DVDs etc., with at least fifty ways to diet and exercise, are 'out there'.

Throughout this book I mention libraries, bookstores; seminars, and workshops as places to find self-help information. Similarly, access to the internet allows you to download e-books, blogs, and periodicals relating to anger management, stress reduction and 'how to' information of numerous kinds.

Look for books on positive thinking, spirituality, marriage, parenting, and money matters. And if vulgar words motivate you (**Hardcore Self-help: F**k Depression by Robert Duff, Ph.D.**), you can find plenty of those books.

Whatever your strategy for improving yourself—be it reading a book, listening to a tape, attending a workshop or a seminar, self-help is the way to go.

SELF-HELP YOURSELF

If the advice you get from a self-help book makes you feel like dirt for even having a problem, take heart, your situation will get better.

I will debunk some widely held myths about what self-help can fix and cannot fix. I will talk down some negative assumptions which some folks already have about self-help. I hope to convince you that it is okay to use a self-help method to address and even perfect an area of your life.

This book will help you to make informed decisions about your personal growth. You do not have to trudge through your own trial and errors to come up with good solutions. You **can** find a teacher within the pages of a self-help book. You will see that it is more convenient to purchase the answers to your concerns than to figure things out for yourself.

Watch other people marvel at your astonishing makeover. They will want to know how you did it. Take action immediately.

Self-help yourself *(Find your "kick-ass" Mentor in a Self-help Book; follow the principles and create your better life)* could be the ideal book for group discussions.

Olive Rose Steele.

CHAPTER ONE

How's your life going?

Balancing work life and social life is not easy. Stress has become the operative daily word for everything that's not 'right' with folks, and a form of therapy usually comes next.

Folks are constantly in search of ways to cope with pressure. Is it any wonder self-help has exploded into the billion dollar industry that it has?

Folks have a fair idea about what they need to improve in themselves. Some aren't comfortable with the self-help doctrine. Nevertheless, it is sensible to 'zero in' on your niggling situation then take remedial steps before the problem becomes worse.

SELF-HELP YOURSELF

What is my purpose? Why is my life not working out as I planned? Where can I get help for my low self-esteem? As long as you are asking yourself these questions you need to consider a form of self-help.

Your emotional state of uncertainty, distress, worry and fear might be the reason your personal success is stymied. If you are overwhelmed with challenges you do not wish to discuss and you are angry all the time, chances are the issues of life are weighing you down.

You probably feel like you are the only person in the entire universe that is experiencing such struggles. Fortunately, that is not true. Many other folks have similar challenges.

If you are anything like I was a few years ago, you might even be questioning your self-worth. Am I good enough? Smart enough? Trustworthy enough? How can I make myself better?

You may have spent too many years in uncomfortable relationships; stuck in dead end jobs and up to your ears in debt.

You're probably saying, I *am who I am, I cannot change.* That is not true. Change is possible for anyone who is serious about change.

OLIVE ROSE STEELE

So you're asking, what *do I do now? Who can I trust?* No worries. Any technique, practice or process used by experts, authors and even amateur writers that educate, and inspire others, is self-help worthy of recognition. Written instructions are published in self-help books which can be found on book shelves. These self-help books address every imaginable situation.

Words and phrases from self-help books can inspire folks and give them hope during moments of self-doubt. Also, family and friends can be generous with advice on how to handle pressing emotional issues.

It is true, the self-help method of making life-changing decisions might not be for everyone but, for those who need 'outside' encouragement, self-help could be the nudge to make that change.

CHAPTER TWO

My story

It is by sheer perseverance and sensible reasoning that I am still married all these decades. In heated debates of the past, I've told my husband I wanted a divorce and his retort was reciprocal. After each discussion, I express regret for my insensitivity only to repeat the performance.

Why was I acting in such a manner, for no good reason? Was I crazy? Decades passed before I realize I was not weird or crazy. My bad attitude was not unlike umpteen other people in committed relationships.

Disagreements will persist because "things" don't always work out to the benefit of one or the other party, and that is a fact of life.

I have had my share of pain, hardships, and ups and downs with complete failures in-between. When times become rocky I have a tendency to put confidence in myself, in the family, relatives, and friends. And when I hit rock bottom I seek God.

At pivotal moments, I have asked myself:

Who do I want to be?

I understand I can **be** who I want to be; I can **do** what I want to do. I recognize I am someone's wife, someone's mother, someone's grandmother, someone's friend, and even someone's sounding board. But is this all I can be?

I truly want to be loving, happy, healthy, wealthy and whole.

Ten years ago I purchased a self-help book titled **The Prophet** by the author, Kahlil Gibran.

The Prophet is my guidebook. It covers my questions concerning religion, love, marriage, relationships, pain and many more questions pertinent to my situation.

The Prophet guided me toward a spiritual pathway. I became an extra sensitive person and a kinder, gentler wife, mother, grandmother and friend.

SELF-HELP YOURSELF

I celebrate my transformation through self-help though I am amaze when people see me and say "How did you do it".

Several versions of every self-help solution, known to humans, have already been written about, talked about, tried, approved of or strongly disapproved of are on record. I will say, however, a self-help book of your choosing is good for your soul.

CHAPTER THREE

What is Self-help?

"Any book is a self-help guide if you can take something from it"
—Kevin Patrick Smith, Author, Speaker

Self-help is knowledge gained through books, audio tapes, CDs, DVDs and the internet to improve the personality of people wishing to make a life change.

Self-help is generally put forward by professionals, specialists and gurus through books, blogs, seminars, workshops, social media, and e-books. This allows the consumer to educate himself or herself about emotional, spiritual, business, and financial lack.

SELF-HELP YOURSELF

Self-help taps into people's desire to be all they can be. The desire to be loved, accepted, wealthy, and good, drives people to seek out experts and gurus for answers to soul searching questions.

Some people believe self-help knowledge is fake and wacky, and the method of distribution, which is through books, audio tapes, CDs, DVDs, workshops, and seminars, etc., is purely for financial gain. Self-help is a way for people to move toward a personal life change. Applying knowledge gained from experts to your situation makes perfectly good sense.

"Why am I angry all the time?" "Why am I not rich like my cousin Susan?" "How can I lose ten pounds in ten days?" "Who stole my cookies from the cookie jar?" These are questions folks struggle with day in and day out. Folks constantly seek answers and, yes, they will get answers to these questions through a self-help method of their choice.

Is my dream attainable? How soon will I achieve my goal? You can find Self-help books, audio tapes, and CDs with advice on ways to achieve success.

Take action. Self-help books are 'out there' that will help you to do well.

I've read books by bestselling authors on a variety of topics about self-improvement. I've attended conferences and workshops and, I've heard personal testimonies from people who've tried self-help and recorded their personal stories.

In my published self-help books; "And When We Pray", "Great is thy Faithfulness" and "The Solid Rock", I share my vulnerabilities; fears, doubts, and insecurities. This allows me to move pass super difficult situations and gets me through challenging emotions, instead of taking them out on someone else. Sharing my vulnerable moments also cultivates a deeper connection with peers and teaches me to come to terms with my sensibilities.

The foundation of my self-help books is my personal relationship with God, Self, and others. For example, in "The Solid Rock", I focus on building relationships. In "And When We Pray", I put forward the use of prayer as an additional spiritual tool that can help people withstand trying life issues. In "Great is Thy Faithfulness", I give examples of how people may recognize when they're going awry in some areas of their life. Not every self-help advice will work out in a perfect way. Self-help will help those people who put what they learn into practice so use self-help as needed.

SELF-HELP YOURSELF

On the other hand, you should be skeptical about a self-help book that touts a faultless outcome in ten days. You are wise to check the credentials of self-help authors. Be practical rather than hypothetical about your challenges as you make inquiries about self-help.

Here are some guiding principles to consider when looking for self-help resources:

Do I need self-help?

Some people stumble on to self-help by chance, meaning an undeniable situation occurs that calls for immediate attention. People don't always know whether or not they need to try a self-help method to address a situation. Many have initially endorsed self-help even though some have returned to their old ways of doing things, out of discouragement. If you are one of those people who say, you are who you are and nothing can change you, then please forgive me when I say you might be missing an opportunity to improve yourself.

Where to find reliable Self-help resources?

Bookstores, Libraries, and the internet are some places where self-help resources can be found. Check journals that have been logged about certain self-help literature.

How to find reliable authors?

Authors of self-help books you choose to read should be practiced in a specific field. I'm not saying they have to have university credentials in psychology to give credible advice, even if such credentials symbolize believability. Authors who are scholastic and steeped in common sense, tend to be truer to life in their delivery. Your neighborhood library is a good place to check for credible self-help authors.

The Dalai Lama, Dr. Wayne Dyer, and Eckhart Tolle are some of my favorite self-help authors. His book titled: "Change the way you look at things and the things you look at change" by Dr. Wayne Dyer, truly inspires me.

How much self-help is enough?

You are depressed. If you are like me, you are feeling weird—like something is 'wrong' with you. You confide in your best girlfriend; she tells you, to your face, that you are acting strange. That's not good.

You'd seen a book about depression advertised on TV. You dash to your local bookstore, to find the book. You hope it will address your circumstances—it might.

SELF-HELP YOURSELF

Don't miss an opportunity to learn and grow. Read a motivational book, attend a workshop or a conference, be part of a support group. Take away everything you believe to be helpful.

Your self-help practice might be the coaching you seek. Experts, gurus and 'novices' are accessible to give advice and opinions, be flexible.

I recommend these self-help books

"The Purpose Driven Life" by Pastor Rick Warren, **"A Return to Love"** by Marianne Williamson**,** "Battlefield of the Mind" by Joyce Meyer, and "One Day My Soul Just Opens Up" by Iyanla Vanzant, are helpful self-help books.

CHAPTER FOUR

Who Needs Self Help?

One myth about self-help is, it is mainly sought after by people in certain economic, intellectual, and emotional circles; often people with a psychological tilt. Though, I found out that anyone, including a new mother who wants to learn how to adequately parent her baby might be interested in related self-help information.

Self-help is not a one-shot deal. People who seek this resource are usually hungry for more information. They know that challenges are wide-ranging and different to each circumstance, so they seek out knowledge that is related to their situations.

You can find trained speakers, thought guides, gurus, and mentors to provide self-help services. They will assist you in your worries and give you good advice.

SELF-HELP YOURSELF

These days, there are new theories and languages relating to the self-help culture. Words such as 'codependency' and phrases like 'family dysfunction' are used to describe certain situations.

These latest descriptions in self-help thinking have now been firmly integrated into mainstream languages and have given gurus and advocates of the self-help thought, new avenues for exploration.

Self-help might be administered through group programs, with its own emphasis, techniques, beliefs, and agendas. It makes little difference how folks pull it together; self-help is the way to go for solutions to manage issues such as anxiety, fear, stress, anger and overall self-improvement. Self-help in all forms is useful.

One aspect of self-help that has served folks well is the use of self-talk; prayers, mantras, and chants. Self-talk, as a linguistic form of self-help, plays a very important role in regulating people's emotions when they experience stress. Self-talk can improve people's ability to normalize their thoughts, feelings, and anxieties in a less threatening manner. And it seems like the folks who practice self-talk see themselves like bystanders thus allowing them to better manage their situations.

Consider the following when deciding which area of self-help will resolve your problem:

- Diet and exercise self-help usually have to do with losing weight or gaining muscle;

- Relationships and breakups self-help assist people in finding the right partner or show them how to deal with splitting up;

- Time management self-help shows folks how to get time back and manage stress from being overworked.

Whether you are a realtor, a carpenter, a restaurant owner, a baggage handler or a day laborer; having good self-help facts might be the difference between you and the individuals you work alongside.

Decide how much self-help you need and how often you need to reach for a book to find information that will help you to cope.

Following are some of the self-help topics people seek out as they self-help themselves:

How to make more money

SELF-HELP YOURSELF

How to be debt free

Unresolved issues

Religion

Spirituality

Wellbeing

Leisure

Do it yourself projects

Fun

How to make more money

People look for opportunities to make quick, legitimate cash. Many are willing to consider schemes delivered through seminars, workshops, books and audio tapes that offer get rich quick ideas.

Learning about wealth accumulation through a self-help technique might attract vulnerable folks; I recommend folks look with critical eyes at all 'get rich quick' schemes.

Whatever your reason to strive for extra cash, ample self-help methods are available. How much extra money folks make depends on how much effort is put into a self-help way of making more money.

OLIVE ROSE STEELE

How to be debt free

People make expensive purchases for cars, homes, and furniture and later regret the decision. For many, a bad financial decision is what puts them in their present fiscal situation. So you ask; how can I be rid of debt?

You are not different from thousands of people who are asking that same question and are looking for ways of becoming debt free.

Most people are not quick to let it slip to family and friends that they're drowning in debt. A situation where creditors are always calling and 'dunning' you to pay a debt you owe is daunting. Such a situation will overwhelm you with fear of every kind. Fear is a wicked emotion.

Debts for a mortgage, your rent, and a medical emergency are unavoidable, however, when we find ourselves in a debt predicament it is wise to budget for a quick repayment.

Rummage through the self-help bookshelf at your local library and bookstore. Find self-help books that give advice on how to live debt free. Read what others have written on the subject. See if what is recommended will guide you to recovery from debt.

SELF-HELP YOURSELF

Unresolved issues

This is tricky. Emotions rise and fall. Emotions play a crucial role in the way people deal with issues that might be difficult to put away. Bad relationship decisions have personal consequences.

Some people believe their unresolved relationship issues are unique to them but thankfully, this is not true. Being alive is the reason you make decisions and being alive is your opportunity to improve on those decisions and even change your mind if you like.

If you find it difficult to admit that you might have played a role in an unresolved situation, take heart, no one is perfect, hurt feelings take a while to rebuild.

Regardless of where you are right now, you can improve yourself. Other people have gone through some of the same crappy things you are going through. Identify your situation and find the right self-help solution.

If it's bothering you, there's a book written about it 'out there'. Out there is brimming with self-help materials to solve all sort problems.

Are you stuck in a career? Are you trying to deal with an out of control child? Still looking to hone a specific job skill? Those situations will prevent you from experiencing good sleep at night. You might be interested in reading a self-help book on how to cure sleep deficiency.

Religion

Religion brings structure and purpose into the lives of many individuals and the Self-help industry integrates religious self-help methods in an amazing way.

Religious Teachers, Pastors, Preachers, experts and Gurus publish their styles of self-help books as add-ons to their teaching and counseling business. Religious self-help books written by popular preachers and teachers could guide souls to faith. Some consumers see this expansion as ideal for self-helping themselves.

Straight-talk Preacher, Bishop T.D. Jakes pulls no punches in his exhortations to his congregation. "Woman Thou Art Loosed" by Jakes is one of his most popular self-help books.

Bishop Jakes' followers rest on every word he says and many of his exhortations appear in his self-help books.

SELF-HELP YOURSELF

Some self-help preachers sell their supporters 'happy feelings' regardless of their dreadful situations and Mega church Pastor, Joel Osteen, immediately comes into my mind. Worshipers are counselled to be peaceful even if the neighbor is difficult towards them.

'Touchy feely' sermons by preachers might be helpful and could be a necessary diversion for some people. However, I caution you, be real in your expectations. Self-help requires an amount of action on your part in order to be meaningful. Folks should consider self-help from a range of sources.

Spirituality

"With spirituality, you embrace the connection between body, mind, and spirit. You acknowledge a Higher Power through worship practices; you build good character as practical ways of living." —Olive Rose Steele

Those on a spiritual path refer to themselves as being on a journey—a journey of self-discovery, enlightenment and faith, and they seek out ways to refine their spiritual nature.

I believe that Spirituality is non-denominational. And the areas of mind and body are hugely popular in the self-help category.

Books with daily prayers and meditations are 'must have' for a lot of folks. "Quiet Mind: One-Minute Retreats from a Busy World" by Author David Kundtz, "The Path to Tranquility: Daily Wisdom by The Dalai Lama" and "Acts of Faith: Meditations for People of Color" by Author Iyanla Vanzant are spiritual self-help books that come to mind.

There are no shortages of information on the subject of spirituality. These self-help guidebooks are prominently displayed in bookstores.

A few years ago, I began a journey of finding my "Self". Prior to that, Church was simply a support system.

Then one day, as I was perusing the aisles of my local bookstore I saw a book titled; *Acts of Faith: Meditations for People of Color* by Author Iyanla Vanzant, and soon after I read her book I began to repeat the daily mantras and practice some of the teachings from her book.

I recognize, if I were going, to be honest with myself and if I were going to be happy, healthy and whole, as I truly desire, then I ought to live the change I want.

I have made phenomenal positive changes and now I share my experiences in all of my published self-help books.

SELF-HELP YOURSELF

Not long ago, my best girlfriend began a journey of spiritual enlightenment. I recommend a few self-help books that I had read. "The Purpose Driven Life" by Pastor and Author Rick Warren was one of them.

Self-help books will invariably look and sound the same even if written by different authors. And the self-help category will remain in the publishing industry for a very long time. Why? Folks look for solutions from sources outside of themselves.

A feature of spirituality is self-talk—prayers, mantras, verses, and phrases. In my own life, I enjoy self-talk during my daily walks. Self-talk is one way in which I verbalize my prayers and regulate stresses.

Another essential part of spirituality is the self-healing techniques for Mind, body, and spirit. People who practice spirituality in their everyday life recognize that self-healing is a path they might follow to achieve a desired result. The more folks practice and use the positive energy they garner, the more self-healing they experience.

And, another key element of spirituality is the ability to use words and actions that might work in a daily routine to self-inspire.

Here's how I self-inspire:

- When I don't feel motivated or enthusiastic I act like I am, and within a short time I actually start to feel enthusiastic;
- when I find self-help writing that speaks to my issues I make it visible to me so that I can refer back during a low period;
- I memorize words and phrases that target my situations in a personal way and I search the scriptures to see what it says concerning my issues;
- I banish fear when it raises its ugly head.

Self-help books on spirituality and managing fear are good to have as reference reading. Most self-help literature provides helpful nuggets for healthy, practical daily survival. I have no doubt; a self-help book can be the catalyst for wholesome living.

Enjoy your healthy, happy, and peaceful spiritual life.

Wellbeing

Do you sleep well? Are you getting along with other people? Are things working out the way you want them? In other words are you happy, healthy, loving and whole?

SELF-HELP YOURSELF

If the answers to the above questions are yes then you are assured of your wellbeing.

Wellbeing means a proper diet. Wellbeing puts folks in a good frame of mind. Wellbeing allows folks to be hopeful. Wellbeing promotes a buoyed disposition. Wellbeing upholds good character and ethical living.

None of the above elements define wellbeing entirely; however, each contributes to it. Wellbeing means naught if folks are not physically and spiritually healthy.

While my ideas about well-being might not be perfect, I believe, wellbeing is how one feels about one's self. Folks are happy, healthy, loving and whole as a consequence of how they feel in a given moment. I encourage you to find self-help resources that speak to your feelings.

Leisure

If you are like me, you often feel rushed, there never seems to be quite enough time to complete the things you need to do.

Folks rarely have time for leisure. Know that leisure time is not sinful. Spa days, retreats, holidays, and sabbatical are leisure activities that may reduce stress, improve health, and increase your life expectancy. Folks can find tutors for lessons in Swimming, Yoga, and Tai Chi.

Meditation, though considered a spiritual act is a leisure activity barring none. Meditation helps in directing awareness toward a particular object. By directing your positive meditative energy to that long overdue Caribbean cruise, you could manifest the cruise much quicker.

Other leisure activities like concerts, performances, musicals, recitals may be included as habits that can help to increase the time you devote to self.

Have a glass of wine, go for a round of golf with your buddies go to the movie theater. See how good you feel.

If you prefer moments of stillness during leisure then "Be still and know..."this is a biblical command to give your mind a break.

Be free to relax and enjoy life your way; however, be mindful of the other folk who do not enjoy the same freedom.

If a friend doesn't drink alcoholic beverage you should avoid consuming in his or her presence.

SELF-HELP YOURSELF

Read self-help articles published in journals that give information about what to do for leisure.

Do-it-yourself projects

Do-it-yourself projects are usually tackled by amateurs and people who use 'how-to' information to finish a project.

Do-it-yourselfers get their 'how-to' information from the local auto mechanic shop, hardware store, and the internet. Information is available on every project for do-it-yourselfers to tackle.

Fun

Fun is the elixir for happiness. Do fun things like skipping work on your birthday; going for a joy ride in your new car and laughing at your own jokes even as others are cranky.

Fun is associated with recreation and play; fun can happen during work, social functions, and even seemingly mundane activities. Having spontaneous fun can contribute to the health of your mind, body, and spirit. If your idea of having fun is just 'kicking back' (relaxing) then do it. Fun that comes through a self-help platform allows folks to practice on their own time at their leisure. It is okay to have fun.

CHAPTER FIVE

Why Self-help?

People who have need of self-help are busy people; they want quick solutions, quick responses and a quick way out. They want solutions for pressing problems, remedies for emotional pain, a useful time management system, a stirring motivational scheme and a realistic goal-setting structure. The self-help solution is one tried and true way of accessing resources 'on the run'.

Since it is good to learn from folks who have already experienced the challenges you face—how they dealt with and overcame the 'isness' of life—then it makes perfectly good sense to 'take a leaf out of their book' so to speak.

Are you afraid your boss or your co-workers might discover a deficiency in your skill?

SELF-HELP YOURSELF

Have you been secretly working on this deficiency? Reading a self-help book? Where is the book stashed? Is it in your purse? Is it in the glove compartment of your car? Is it in the bottom drawer of your desk at the office? Take heart, you're not a weirdo.

Somewhere in those folded pages of your hidden self-help book, you could find concrete steps and a workable blueprint for a realistic turning point in your life.

While it is true that some people are skeptical about the concept of self-help, many have testified to the help they receive through a self-help system.

When you realize your challenges are not different from umpteen other people, you can relate and even be concerned about other people's plight. Get self-help information from experts who have the answers.

Folks have been disappointed with 'fail proof guarantees' made by self-help authors and gurus. Be leery of guarantees but don't give up on your search for answers to what angst you.

Self-help, as a motivational/inspirational resource, requires action on your part. Know that it is unrealistic to believe that self-help, in any form, is merely to define your life's dreams.

OLIVE ROSE STEELE

I will tell you, the self-help industry is saturated with educational resources. This market will continue to sustain itself because folks are looking for solutions which are essential to their wellbeing.

CHAPTER SIX

When do I need Self-help?

'Don't rely on someone else for your happiness and self-worth. Only you can be responsible for that. If you can't love and respect yourself – no one else will be able to make that happen. Accept who you are – completely; the good and the bad – and make changes as YOU see fit – not because you think someone else wants you to be different."
– Stacey Charter

In this Chapter, I will address self-help that inspires personal growth. Following are some reasons you might need self-help.

- **When life throws a 'monkey wrench' into your plans**

You may not be happy with your present circumstances. You are probably rethinking your routine after a divorce, a devastating financial meltdown, loss of your home to foreclosure, your car repossessed, and a sudden illness that threw a monkey wrench into your plans. You think this might be the right time to turn over a new leaf although you're not ready to make drastic changes.

You are probably tangled up in issues like regrets, discouragements and humiliations and your approach in dealing with those issues might be the same as in the past; meaning you leave such matters to happenstance.

Your stuff needs your attention even if you are not able to sort out all of it immediately. Some stuff may take a longer time to complete. If you are convinced some of your stuff needs to be reorganized do it now. Check out the self-help aisle of your bookstore; see what the experts have written about the issue in question.

Religious people should check out books and audio tapes that are available at their places of worship and even consider secular self-help books.

The 'monkey wrench' that life may have thrown in your plans could be to alert you that it is time to make a life adjustment.

Are you happy with what is going on in your life? Buy a self-help book that speaks to the question. Read up on how to be happy.

SELF-HELP YOURSELF

- *When you make a decision to be honest with self*

People want to make something of themselves and one way they do this is, by being honest about their desires. Your honesty is what makes you decide on the right plan for your self-help needs.

- *When there's tension that needs your attention*

The Tension you're feeling might not even be your 'business'. Pressure can come from spouse, family, children and friends, and can land on your lap for your attention. You feel tension when you need to change a course or do something different about your situation.

Ask yourself: Which self-help method would be appropriate in my moment of tension? Where can I go for help? Where can I find a therapist, a guru, an expert or a Pastor to help me? A self-help book could be the springboard to a successful remedy.

Meditations, group discussions, and social connections during periods of tension are good therapy. Recognize tension and give it your attention. Any self-help book that targets your issues, makes you see clearly and guides you to solutions, is worth reading.

- ***When your solutions no longer work***

Some people resolve their issues by showing a good-looking self-image. They may search for a better job, purchase a luxury car, take a vacation and even extend the family by adding a cat. Still, the anxiety attacks keep occurring.

If what you've been doing no longer works, teach yourself a new way with self-help. Self-help could be a less expensive solution. Read an empowering book; one that comes to my mind is "Excuses Begone: How to Change Lifelong, Self-Defeating Thinking" by Author Dr. Wayne Dwyer.

Do I need self-help? You ask. It may surprise you to know that more and more people are applying a form of self-help in their everyday living.

Self-help information is worth reaching for when your solutions are not working for you. You will find that every time you read a self-help book you discover 'something' that speaks to your circumstances. For example, the story about a man who died, went to heaven, and came back to life to tell about it; a woman who overcame a major disability and became a great gymnast; and a boy who 'beat' terminal illness, are stories that later turn into inspirational self-help books.

CHAPTER SEVEN

Where does Self-help come from?

"The desire to savor life is, I believe, what drives many of us to the self-help aisle in the first place. Most of us are not suffering a real addiction, not crippled by low self-esteem, not battling repressed memories: ... What really drives us to seek help is an equally frightening sensation: that of being alive, yet not really living."—Dr. Paul Pearsall.

The Self-help concept has been around for many centuries; some say about three or four centuries. Apparently, the idea started by experts of that time to educate lay people who yearned for information about issues like weight loss, parenting, marriage, etiquette, success, self-control, grief, self-medicine and so on. Since then the self-help industry continues to grow in leaps and bounds.

Oprah Winfrey, Marianne Williamson, Iyanla Vanzant, Wayne Dyer, Tony Robins, Deepak Chopra, Bishop T.D. Jakes, Joyce Meyer and many more well-known Authors/Inspirational Speakers continue to put pen to paper, market, and distribute millions of self-help books that net millions of dollars.

People's desire is to learn the 'whys' and 'wherefores' of how to achieve, and many feel it is easier to learn from those who already 'made it' and has written about it.

Any, if not all areas of our life can be improved with information from an expert with sound advice. And the answers we get could be just what we need in our moments of questioning.

Experts, like Robert Duff, Ph.D., use strong words in their books to ignite folks. I find the contents of Dr. Duff's book *"Hardcore Self-help: F**k Depression"* to be candid and super helpful, yet very amusing.

Take advantage of a 'kick ass' mentor in a self-help book, follow his or her solutions and improve your situation. You can even talk back to this 'kick-ass' mentor without being punished or disciplined.

Folks tend to expect immediate change. Be patient.

SELF-HELP YOURSELF

The ten-day positive result that a stress management self-help book advertises might be too short a period to work for you. Don't give up, you have the formula. Keep working at it.

Would you like to win and keep friends? There are books that will teach you how.

Would you like to influence other people? Check the self-help aisle at your local bookstore or library. Are you looking for a book on wellness? Find one in your local grocery store.

One way to feel better about self and life is by reading a good book, especially one that gets to the point. For example, the self-help book: "Think and Grow Rich" by Author Napoleon Hill, is still relevant to thousands.

"How to Win Friends & Influence People" by Author Dale Carnegie, is another original self-help book of consequence that continues to serve many in a positive way.

Would you like to improve your sex life? The self-help industry is heavy with information on the subject of sexual health. There are plenty guidebooks in bookstores, and on the internet.

CHAPTER EIGHT

Self-help should NOT be...

Self-help should not be a reason to be ignorant about your reality: The webinar you participated in says you are a millionaire if you think you are, because you are what you believe.

In reality, people know that a millionaire is usually one who works long, hard and smart at a business enterprise or organization that he or she created, which brought in enormous amounts of money.

Nothing is wrong with building a dream—dreams become real when you take big positive steps toward bringing forward those dreams.

SELF-HELP YOURSELF

Self-help is not a reason to think your life will finally be without pain or suffering if you follow the advice of an expert or guru. Self-help should certainly not be a way to 'stick your head in the sand'.

Self-help should not be a last resort: Don't turn to self-help when all else fails for you might go to the wrong seminars and workshops, and, you might not purchase the self-help books that are right for you—know that self-help is not a one size fits all experiment.

Self-help should not be purely for personal satisfaction: If your self-development does not influence the people you are associated with, then you might want to reconsider your need to self-help yourself.

Self-help should not be substituted for inaction: Self-help requires action on your part. Learn from the self-help you choose and put it in practice.

Self-help is not meant to make you addicted.

Self-help is not meant for you to live vicariously through an expert, a therapist, a guru or someone else's success. In these days of quick and instant, it might be expedient to follow the teachings of an expert; however, don't be a self-help junkie.

CHAPTER NINE

Self-help SHOULD be...

Investment in Self-help material should be money well spent: The truth is everyone who reads a book, listens to an audio tape or CD and attends a workshop should absorb something from the exercise.

Some people purchase self-help literature just because they attended a conference or workshop and many never read the material after that. Invest in self-help literature that you plan to keep for future reference. Most self-help literature adds value.

Self-help should end on a positive note: The self-help book you purchased that gives 12 things you must do to improve your self-esteem is on your bookshelf ...set aside time to read, and re-read that book.

SELF-HELP YOURSELF

I admit that some recommendations are virtually hard to follow or even keep up with. For example, the advertised 10-day and 30-day programs to shed ten pounds are often unattainable. Be good to yourself, follow the advice as best you can.

Self-help should inspire at the 'end of the day': Self-help literature should give a feeling of having accomplished something; a belief that you honor your desire to improve yourself and you can become a better person. A good self-help book should give you an emotional boost yet not make you complacent. The feel good part of self-help should show up after you have accomplished a task.

Every do-it-yourself project, good and bad financial decision, and, unresolved relationship issue is thought of and decided on by experts, gurus and lay people. Inform yourself. Heck, if it's not self-help then its 'chicken soup', take advantage of what's available?

You don't have to shell out a lot of money to get answers to what's holding you back. Expect to be advised on the best course of action by a self-help method. You are who will be doing the hard work of improving yourself.

CHAPTER TEN

"We cannot change what we are not aware of, and once we are aware, we cannot help but change."

—Sheryl Sandberg, Author

I call this chapter STUDY UP.

Life is not easy—never meant to be. It has its ups and downs, and peaks and valleys. People are constantly looking for answers; likely from trusted channels.

We live in what is known as the 'information age'. Everything we want to know is somewhere on the internet, written in a book and taught by an expert. The challenge we face is figuring out the authenticity of the information we get.

SELF-HELP YOURSELF

Follow the suggestions I put forward in this book and self-help yourself.

At this point, I'd like to congratulate you. It seems to me like you have considered the self-help route. You spent some time in bookstores, searching for books, audio tapes, CDs, everything that corresponds with your need to know. You are repeating words and phrases that inspire you. This is no time to pull back—get more self-help information.

You have a good sense of the area of your life that needs to be fixed. You are taking a long hard look at your choices; you are ready to do what it takes to make a life change.

You are facing down some fears that have been dogging you. You signed up at the gym. You are proud of yourself.

The self-help book that popped out at you from the shelf at the bookstore, titled "100 days to a sexy new body - Yours" grabbed your attention. You know this is the self-help book for you. This is your opportunity to take a new stance about your appearance. You inhale and exhale. Then you immerse yourself in the book. You believe it will help you solve your problem.

Hurray!

Now you will put some things into practice. You unload some stuff that had been holding you back. You banish fear into oblivion where it belongs.

Instead of focusing on the wants and needs of other people, you are being responsible for yourself. You are less preoccupied about other people's business. You are tending to your emotional needs instead of leaving your needs to the whim of other people. You recognize that me, myself and I are one and the same.

Past mistakes are just that, past. Your inclination is no longer to look back with regret. You are **not** being selfish but if you are, that is a good thing! You are developing into a new person. You can be yourself without apologizing.

The self-help book you purchased was worth the price you paid for it!

Study up on the Fear Factor

Fear will try to keep you linked to your past in a wounded way, banish fear. Fear is no longer your Achilles heel.

People who self-educate through self-help shouldn't hesitate to update themselves. A new book, a motivational conference, an inspirational workshop and fresh audio tapes should be at the top of your list of essentials.

I am not suggesting you read self-help books at all times, I am saying, get the updates you need for your circumstances and when in doubt go back to the Bible for it contains everything you need to self-help yourself.

Study up on your personality

Your personality might be the reason you've been in a funk for such a long time, don't put obstacles between you and the job promotion you desire. Self-help methods are available to change you into a perfect individual.

Study up on confidence in 'You'

Don't say: I am not smart like my fellow workers; I am not beautiful like my sister Rosa; I will never have long hair; nobody likes me. You are one of a kind. You are the best you can be. Inspire yourself with positive words.

CHAPTER ELEVEN

You got it!

"If you are the type of person to carry a lot of worries, especially about unfinished business, you are also probably the type to feel really guilty when you do things other than those pieces of unfinished business. Guilt is such a shitty thing. As if things weren't hard enough with the anxiety symptoms, guilt just creeps right up in there and makes things exponentially more difficult. I like to call this snowballing. You get worked up and then getting worked up makes you feel bad and then you get more worked up about feeling bad about getting worked up and then.... you get the point."
— Robert Duff, Ph.D. Psychology

Within the pages of many self-help books, you will find information to raise your self-esteem and boost your confidence; instructions to grow you into a good wife, husband, mother, child, sibling, relative, friend, and colleague.

SELF-HELP YOURSELF

You can look beyond disparagements and caustic remarks that people level at you. You can be happy, you can be healthy, you can be wealthy, you can be loving, and you can be whole.

You are probably waiting to read my ten or twenty steps to a satisfactory self-help plan. I have no such plan. Experts, authors, and gurus have written self-help books that have satisfied, rescued, inspired and motivated millions of people. Some self-help books, audio tapes, CDs, and DVDs have become famous bestselling items. Get the products which are relevant to your situation.

Throughout this book, I've given you my suggestions and insights. Some of them are written in my own self-help books. I hope my suggestions will help you in your search for self-help that speaks to your situation. If you follow what I laid out I am certain you will gather the courage to take bold steps toward a changed life; I give you my word!

Now it's your Turn. Take action.

Purchase a self-help book, an audio tape, a CD or a DVD.

Attend a seminar or a workshop and if all else fails, listen to someone's story, you may find the helpful information you've been looking for.

ABOUT THE AUTHOR

Olive Rose Steele resides with her Husband, Herbert, in Ontario, Canada. She writes motivational/inspirational books with Novels and a Memoir mixed in. Her interests range from reading to writing. She's also interested in politics. She adores her granddaughters and enjoys volunteering.

Please check out **The View from my Coffee Cup,** my monthly Blog, posted at WordPress: oliverosesteele.wordpress.com.
E-mail: oliverose29@yahoo.com
www.about.me/oliverose29
www.amazon.com/e/B004W80S8W
Twitter: @olive_steele

OTHER BOOKS BY OLIVE ROSE STEELE

And When We Pray
(Suggestions and Prayers for living in Spirit)

Great is thy Faithfulness
(Insights for Seekers of Self)

The Solid Rock
(Other ground is sinking sand)

Cry Tough
(A Novel)

Watt Town Road
(As Memoir)

Made in the USA
Middletown, DE
09 September 2023

37787129R00035